D1630186

£4.25

Written and edited by Kesta Desmond. Layout and design by Louise Ivimy. Photographs supplied by *All Action Photographic, Retna Pictures, Syndication International* and *World Press Network.*

Published by,
GRANDREAMS LTD.
Jadwin House, 205/211 Kentish Town Road,
London. NW5 2JU.

Printed in Belgium.

ISBN 0 86227 7876.

CONTENTS

"If you make a show with twee children who are dressed up and saying twee little middle class things then it will have no cultural relevance and therefore the kids just won't watch it!"

These are the words of *Home and Away's* original producer, Alan Bateman, and since he spoke them, *Home and Away* has gathered a cult following in the UK as well as in Australia and although many things have been said about it, it has never been accused of being `middle class' or `twee'. So Alan Bateman can sit back, loosen his tie and relax!

Neighbours - A Hard Act To Follow!

At the outset, *Home and Away was* something of a gamble. After the meteoric success of *Neighbours* and the global obsession with Kylie Minogue and Jason Donovan it was clearly a hard act to follow. But *Neighbours* is not without its critics and the people who pioneered *Home and Away* scrutinised their criticisms and turned them to their own advantage.

SOAP

For instance, the most popular objection to life on Ramsay Street is that it has nothing to do with *real* Australian life. Secondly, if you look at any one episode nothing much actually *happens!* In *Neighbours* the definition of a cliff-hanger is the dithering Harold Bishop falling off his exercise bicycle! As Ray Kolle, who handles the *Neighbours* script argues: "We are often tempted to use a sensational story but usually we pull back and say, 'That's not likely to happen.'"

From Teenage Pregnancy To Drugs!

Now, *Home and Away* script writers have turned all this on its head. The plot lines are fast moving and the stories are never shy of scandal and intrigue. In its time the soap has covered such potent issues as teenage pregnancy, unemployment, drugs and alcoholism.

"I wanted to make an Australian drama that dealt with the hopes, aspirations and fears of young people," says Bateman.

But how was the idea of a foster home arrived at? As with all the best drama, *Home and Away* is derived from a real life situation. As Alan Bateman was driving through New South Wales several years ago he happened upon a town that was bitterly divided by the arrival of a centre for homeless children. The situation caught his imagination and he became interested in the whole idea of fostering and said, "I knew then that I had found my theme."

The Search For A Cast!

Months of research in which writers worked with real foster children turned into years, until finally, the first finished script arrived on the producer's desk. What followed then, was a painstaking search for a cast. In order to find the younger characters, casting directors sat through an awesome three hundred and fifty auditions. As series producer, John Holmes said, "It was a slow and exacting process and it needed tremendous patience. *Home and Away* reflects that process because I think the casting in it is superb!"

Now, *Home and Away* has been on our screens in the UK for well over a year and it continues to gain momentum so that it not only rivals the Aussie *Neighbours* but presents a sunnier alternative to British soaps!

INTRODUCING THE

CHARACTERS

*T*om Fletcher (played by Roger Oakley).
Tom Fletcher is the raison d'etre for the Summer Bay foster home. When he and his wife, Pippa, find out that they cannot have children, Tom suggests that they try fostering instead. Having been fostered as a child himself Tom is particularly keen to put his idea into practice. It turns out to be a success. Tom is a doting father and shares his attention equally among `his' children.

*P*ippa Fletcher
(played by Vanessa Downing).
Pippa is Tom's wife and billed as the perfect mother. It is somewhat ironic that after Pippa gives up her career to take care of the foster kids she becomes pregnant herself.

*F*rank Morgan (played by Alex Papps). ▶
Frank was Tom and Pippa's original foster child. After he is coaxed away from a life of crime by the Fletchers he enjoys a relatively stable home life. That is, until his encounter with Roo - a love affair that nearly ends in tragedy. Nowadays though, Frank is happily married to the character of Bobby.

*B*obby Simpson
(played by Nicolle Dickson).
Bobby is variously described as a loner, a juvenile delinquent and a rebel. Her relationships with other members of the Summer Bay residents have always been stormy, particularly where Roo and Carly are concerned. But thanks to the combined influence of Tom, Pippa and Frank, she has mellowed somewhat.

*S*ally Keating (played by Kate Ritchie). Sally is the youngest of the Fletchers' foster children. At the age of three her parents were killed in a boating accident and, after living with her grandmother for a while, Sally was taken into a home. She survived this unhappy time of her life by retreating into a fantasy world of imaginary friends. But help came in the form of a real life friend, Lynn, who shared a dormitory with Sally. When Lynn Lynn came to be adopted by the Fletchers she refused to leave the home unless Sally went with her. Tom and Pippa agreed and the two girls moved into Summer Bay.

*C*arly Morris ▲ (played by Sharyn Hodgson). Carly's life has been far from easy. She was battered by her father as a child and as a result was fostered out to Tom and Pippa. As a teenager her life has been dogged with problems, not least of which have been an attack which led to alcoholism. She is described as vivacious but probably her strongest trait is her tendency to stretch the truth!

*S*teven Matheson (played by Adam Willits). Steven came to the Fletchers after his parents were killed in a fire. For a long time he was severely disturbed by the bereavement but gradually time has diluted the memories and nowadays Steven enjoys the life of the average teenager.

*A*ilsa Stewart (played by Judy Nunn). Ailsa Hogan was running the Summer Bay grocery store when she met Alf Stewart. Although she was a newcomer to the place he and the other locals made her welcome. Now, by virtue of her marriage to Alf she is an integral member of the community. She is described as "warm hearted and generous to a fault" and she is always prepared to leap to the defence of a friend. Bobby in particular.

*A*lf Stewart ▲ (played by Ray Meagher).
Alf is father to the scheming Roo and now husband to the kind hearted Ailsa. His first wife was killed in a drowning accident in 1985; Alf and Roo carried on living in the family home until Alf found the memories of his wife too painful to bear. At that point they sold the house to the Fletchers.

*R*uth Stewart (played by Justine Clarke).
`Roo' is the much-hated character who attempts to sabotage her father's marriage to Ailsa and who nearly fools Frank into marrying her by claiming that she is carrying his baby. There are two sides to her personality; to the adults she is charming and personable. To people of her own age she is boy-crazy and scheming.

*D*onald Fisher ▲ (played by Norman Coburn).
Donald is the headmaster at Summer Bay High School. He is principled and authoritarian and widely disliked because of it. He realises this and feels resentful that what he sees as his good work in the community goes unrecognised.

*C*elia Stewart (played by Fiona Spence).
Celia is the younger sister of Alf and, unlike him, she has never married. She is a stereotypical spinster and busybody. She fills her bitter life with gossip; she is a keen church-goer and a fervent supporter of Donald Fisher!

*M*artin Dibble (played by Craig Thomson).
Martin is something of a beach bum. He is under the false impression that he is Summer Bay's `hottest property' and even when women don't respond to his `charms' his confidence remains undented.

*L*ance Smart (played by Peter Vroom).
`Smart' is the least appropriate name for this guy. He is Martin's partner in crime and definitely the more slow witted of the pair.

*B*rett and Stacey Macklin (played by Gerry Sont and Sandie Lillingston). ▶
These two are brother and sister *and* business partners. They are the offspring of influential property developer, Gordon Macklin and originally, their job was to negotiate the rights to build a leisure complex at Summer Bay. While Stacey is the cool-headed business woman, Brett is continually engaged in a struggle to live up to his father's expectations. Brett is the father to Roo's adopted baby.

*M*att Wilson (played by Greg Benson). Matt is described as the `hunky beach boy' of Summer Bay. He wears a permanent tan and is most at home on a surf board! ▼

*F*loss and Neville McPhee (played by Sheila Kennelly and Frank Lloyd).
Floss and Neville are the retired residents of the Summer Bay caravan park. Despite the fact that they constantly bicker over money - Floss would give anything to anyone - they are still in love after thirty five years of marriage. ▼

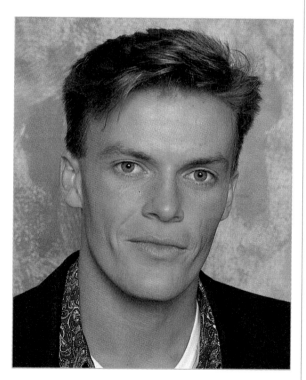

*D*r. Phillip Matheson (played by John Morris).
Phillip turns up in Summer Bay as the long lost uncle of Steven. Although he only intended a short stay he is now working in a local hospital and is romantically involved with Stacey Macklin.

Question Time

STEVEN

Q. Where did he spend his childhood?
A. *In a Sydney suburb called Hornsby?*

Q. How old is he?
A. *Seventeen.*

Q. What is Adam's screen character, Steven Matheson like?
A. *He started off as a bit of a bookworm but as he has grown up he has found distractions more engaging than academia!*

Q. What was his greatest Home and Away moment?
A. *Kissing Narelle! (Played by Amanda Newman-Phillips). Apparently as soon as Adam got his hands on the script he scanned the pages to find out how many kissing scenes he had. "In the script I had this plan to get Narelle to kiss me, because I'd done a survey and I'm a pretty hot kisser. It wasn't as though we were in love though!"*

Q. What's the best thing about being in Home and Away?
A. *The money, which allows Adam to go out and "enjoy himself!"*

Q. When did Adam begin acting?
A. *When he was nine years old.*

Q. What did he appear in?
A. *Marbles; All My Sons; Anna, Damsels Be Damned; Weekend of the Lonesome Rustler and Mad Max III.*

ADAM

Q. Looking back, does Adam have any regrets?
A. *On the whole - no. But he reckons that if he could turn back the clock he wouldn't be a child actor again. "I would quite happily go back to school and take it from there," he says.*

Q. What's the worst thing about being in Home and Away?
A. *"Getting recognised everywhere I go."*

Q. Has Adam visited Britain?
A. *Yes! As well as living in London for a year, Adam paid a promotional visit to the capital earlier on in 1990. He currently holds a British passport as well as an Australian one.*

Q. What does he think of London?
A. *The pigeons in Trafalgar Square give him the creeps; the burgers make him feel sick; the weather makes him want to jump back on a plane but he likes the shops and he enjoyed being on Wogan!*

Q. What does Adam hope for in the future?
A. *"I want to keep healthy, get fit, eat well ... and I want to fall in love!"*

Q. Does he have anyone in mind?
A. *Not right now!*

Q. What sort of fan mail does he receive?
A. *"I guess I get all sorts of stuff. Fans tell me about themselves, what they like about the show, I even get to hear about their problems sometimes. I get a lot of letters from girls in Britain!"*

WILLITS

" Britain's good once you get used to the freezing cold and the time change! "

13

"Glamour and things like that don't do anything for me."

SHARYN HODGSON

CARLY

AGE: 21.

HOME:
Panania; a suburb of Sydney. "No one's ever heard of it," says Sharyn.

PREVIOUS JOB:
"I worked in my dad's shop. It was boring me to death."

FAMILY:
Sharyn has a younger brother who is also in the acting profession and a sister who is still at school.

PETS:
A dog!

ALTERNATIVE CAREER:
"I've always wanted to be an archaeologist."

FAVOURITE BAND:
The Smiths.

FAVOURITE FOOD:
Seafood.

SPORTS:
Swimming.

WORST FEAR:
Cockroaches!

HOBBIES:
Painting and drawing.

FAVOURITE MOVIE:
Stand By Me.

ACTING AMBITIONS:
"I'd like to do something challenging - a film or a stage production that I could work on for a period of time."

■ She was educated at Sydney University and after graduating she went on to do a masters degree in English Literature.

■ Her first ever television role was in a programme called *The Restless Years*.

■ At just fourteen, Vanessa joined the Australian Theatre for Young People. She says she spent every weekend there rehearsing for future productions and claims that she can't remember a time when she didn't want to act!

ALL ABOUT
VANESSA DOWNING
PIPPA

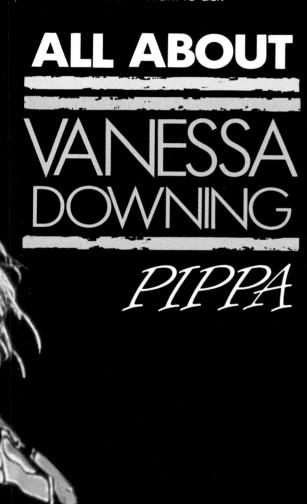

■ Vanessa is married to Australian theatre director, Rodney Fisher. They met five years ago when Vanessa was working for a theatre company.

■ She has a healthy cynicism about soap operas! "I don't have much time for the endless stream of murders, blackmail and silly love stories that you find on some soaps. The events in *Dynasty* are ridiculous!" Her attitude towards *Home and Away* is predictably more lenient; "*Home and Away* is a slice of real life - it's a show with real characters and real stories!"

■ Several years ago Vanessa was out of work for a ten month period. In desperation she joined the Sydney Philharmonic Choir! "It literally saved me from depression. Group singing is really therapeutic!" she says.

■ Vanessa wasn't the first choice for the part of Pippa Fletcher. Instead, Carol Willesse, ex model and wife of a popular TV host was selected. Carol lasted two days before she was fired for her lack of experience. At this point casting directors gave Vanessa's agent a call!

■ Vanessa's past theatrical and screen experience has been quite diverse and has included parts in *Who's Afraid Of Virginia Woolf*, *The Threepenny Opera* and *Sons and Daughters*!

■ When Vanessa was contacted by the *Home and Away* team with the news that she had got the part she was singing in a six piece a cappella group called *The Madrigirls*! Even when she took up the part she carried on singing so that sometimes she was working a twenty hour day.

■ The youngest character part that Vanessa has played was a girl of seventeen, the oldest was "a sixty five year old derelict woman".

JOHN MORRIS

PHILLIP MATHESON

Home and Away has captured a young following of viewers: the cast is young and the issues are relevant to a young audience. Producers were more than happy with this but in order to 'up' the age of the average viewer they introduced the character of Dr. Phillip Matheson played by John Morris. As Alan Bateman said; "What we've been trying to do is introduce elements that will appeal to the eighteen plus age group."

John Morris may well have been successful here. However, like Alex Papps, he is quick to shun the heart throb tag. "I just feel proud to have got the part," he says.

John was among 150 actors who auditioned for the part and it was his first major television role. Beforehand the total extent of his experience had been doing TV commercials and radio and theatre voice overs. He was thrilled with the break: "I'm rapt in the opportunity that I've been given. This is the biggest role I could have landed."

John considers himself even more fortunate due to the fact that he had a near fatal accident less than a year before he auditioned for the Home and Away part. As he alighted from a train his foot became jammed in the door and as the train gathered speed John was dragged along with it. It was just in the nick of time that he managed to free himself.

"I've been lucky in my life and my career," John says. "Well, maybe it's not so much luck as through being myself and knowing that good things would happen if I hung in there."

When John is away from the Summer Bay sets his two main hobbies are football and surfing. He is an Australian Rules Player with Sydney's Paddington club.

FAMOUS NEW ARRIVALS:

DANNII, TERRY & CRAIG

Kylie Minogue's sister is coming to Summer Bay! Nineteen year old Dannii Minogue has decided to follow in the footsteps of her big sister and seek stardom the soap way! Already Dannii has made her name musically in Australia and she has a catalogue of TV appearances behind her, including *The Sullivans* and *Young Talent Time*. Series producer of *Home and Away*, Andrew Howie, has the following to say: "Dannii is a highly talented young lady, I think she will do well... with or without Kylie."

Dannii joined the soap in Australia late in 1989 and it won't be long before her character: the troublesome `Emma', hits our screens too!

Another newcomer with a famous relative is Terence Donovan, the father of Jason! Terence may be unknown in this country but in Australia his name is household property! Even when Jason was in nappies, Terence was appearing in such perennial favourites as *Division 4* and *Cop Shop*. Now, he makes his debut on *Home and Away* as the dastardly Al Simpson and it seems a fair prediction that he won't get anything like the adulation that Jason does!

Terry says of his latest part: "It's a great role. I'm a jail bird, a wife beater and a drunk. But I'll play him as a lovable villain!"

Terry's first scenes in *Home and Away* were shot on October 23rd of last year but on the day that he discovered that he had landed the role Jason was thousands of miles away in England. Said Terry: "I knew what his reaction would be. I told him on the phone and he said, `That's cool'".

If the faces of Dannii and Terry are not familiar then the face of Craig McLachlan almost certainly will be. Craig was the actor who was behind the rogueish character of Henry Ramsay on rival soap *Neighbours*, and since he has left Ramsay Street he has changed drastically! Gone are the long blond locks and gone are the madcap schemes and practical jokes. Instead, we have a cool and mature school teacher called Grant Mitchell.

After Craig's portrayal of Henry as the wacky, fun loving, come what may layabout, the character of Grant comes as a bit of a shock. What, you may wonder, were Craig's reasons for leaving a soap that creates megastars as fast as you can say Stock, Aitken and Waterman!?

" I could never give up the acting. I'm too much of a poser! "

Apart from the fact that a large fee was involved, Craig reckons that he had had his fill of Henry Ramsay: "After being in *Neighbours* for three years Henry became... not easy to play, but I knew where I was with the character. It's a terrific experience for me to expand into other areas and this time I'm playing a more serious role. I've had to make a conscious effort to drop any `Henryisms'. So it's been fun in that respect.

"Grant really digs teaching and his pupils. He's not a Robin Williams / *Dead Poet's Society* clone but he's certainly unorthodox."

Leaving *Neighbours* was tough, however. On Craig's last day his fellow *Neighbours* stars demonstrated their lasting affection for him by smothering him with shaving cream and confetti. Through cream coated lips Craig concluded: "It's been a very emotional day for me!"

Sharyn Hodgson & Matt Stephenson

JUSTINE CLARKE &

SHARYN HODGSON

TWO TOUGH ROLES

In *Neighbours,* when Scott and Charlene were married they returned home to live with Charlene's mum and subjects such as having kids or pregnancy were outlawed from the script with a fastidiousness that even Mrs Mangel would approve of! Not so on *Home and Away!* Take Roo for example: she not only became pregnant while she was still a teenager but her baby was born illegitimately!

RISQUE STUFF!

For an early evening show that many people once classified as a kid's programme, this was risque stuff! However, producers and cast alike realise the implications of the storylines and what viewers don't see is the research and preparation that goes into every role.

In the case of Roo, the actress behind the character, Justine Clarke, knew nothing about the state of being pregnant or how to give a convincing portrayal of child birth. "Getting pregnant was the last thing on my mind," she says!

LENTILS!

The actual scenes in which Roo was noticeably pregnant did not present too much of a challenge: she had to wear a bag filled with lentils beneath her clothes and as episodes passed the amount of lentils was increased!

However, the giving birth scenes proved more difficult but, fortunately for Justine, the wife of one of *Home and Away*'s directors, had recently had a child and her complicated labour replicated the *Home and Away* plot almost exactly.

HYPERVENTILATION!

"I went to her house," explains Justine, "and the two of us sat there doing breathing exercises for two hours at a time!" In addition to this, Justine watched videos of child birth and read all the right books! But, as she said, "When it actually came down to it I still wasn't really prepared, I knew everything about having a baby but I didn't know what the physical pain was like. It felt strange!"

Justine had to play about fifteen scenes where she was actually in labour. "I got a bit dizzy because I had to breathe so much. Then I started to hyperventilate. It was a long day," she concludes.

ALCOHOLISM!

Another Summer Bay actress who has become notorious for playing difficult or controversial roles is Sharyn Hodgson, better known as Carly. This is the character who was battered as a child and raped as a teenager and who ultimately turned to alcohol for solace.

The post-rape scenes caused something of a stir in Britain. The censorious Mary Whitehouse was heard to say, "Scenes like this are unnecessary... terrible and highly irresponsible." Parents up and down the country were meanwhile putting pens to paper. But as Sharyn argues, if something happens in real life why should it be excluded from television?

REALISM!

"In *Home and Away* we show life as it really happens. It's not irresponsible to have attacks, unwanted pregnancies or people turning to alcohol. It's realistic and in the show we're confronting these problems."

When Sharyn embarked on the role she obviously had no experience of being a rape survivor or of being an alcoholic: "I do know people who drink, but no one with an alcohol problem."

RESEARCH!

So, like Justine, she set about the painstaking process of researching her role: "I read articles and watched documentaries so that it would be believable. For advice about the attack scenes I called the Rape Crisis Centre and I read case histories. I knew how someone would feel... you'd hate yourself and feel that *you* had done the wrong thing."

When Sharyn had completed the scenes she said, "There were lots of occasions where Carly had to break down and cry. I felt drained after that!"

The *Papps* & *Dickson*

Mini-book

THE LIFE AND TIMES OF

> " I feel very lucky, but I never take anything for granted. It could all go tomorrow. "

ALEX PAPPS

career, "I was bright but I guess I was lazy."

The Reluctant Actor...
On leaving school Alex decided that his future lay in photography. He went on a media production course and the world of acting couldn't have been further from his mind. Although his parents - both school teachers - were actively involved in a theatre group, no amount of coaxing on their part would persuade him to tread the boards. Alex was definitely `a props man'.

Then one day, he changed his mind. He laid down his props, emerged from the wings and gave it his all on stage. "I loved it", he says in amazement. "I loved every minute of it!"

Growing Up in the Dandenongs...
Alex Papps' life before *Home and Away* was, by all accounts, pretty normal. He was the first son of Richenda and Apollo Papps and he was born on the 11th February, 1969.

The birth of sister, Selena, two years later, marked the completion of the Papps family. They lived and grew up in the Dandenongs, just an hour's drive from Alex's birth place, Melbourne, and Alex passed an unremarkable school

From *Prisoner Cell Block H* to *The Flying Doctors*...
After this there was no stopping him. He went on to appear in *Ready or Not*, *Prisoner Cell Block H*, *The Henderson Kids*, *Neighbours*, *The Factory*, and then came the part that launched him into

30

serious fame: Frank Morgan in *Home and Away*.

Thanks to that part, Alex is now something of a heart throb - a title he regards with healthy disdain: "It's something I can't really relate to. I know who I am and I'm not that hyped up person you see on TV. I'm the sort of person who dags around at home, watches television and orders home delivery pizza."

Now, of course Alex has cast aside his Frank Morgan persona and flown the *Home and Away* nest only to make a comfortable landing in *The Flying Doctors*. On leaving *Home and Away* he said, "I'd like to do something different... something which will mean my next step up. The danger in staying in a soap too long is that people start seeing you as that character."

And the series producer of *The Flying Doctors* is none other than Alan Bateman! Says Bateman, "Alex will be a character in the town of Coopers Crossing. It will be a very different role to that of Frank - much more mature."

As far as Alex himself is concerned, the fact that he has defected to Coopers Crossing means that he has been able to move back from Sydney to Melbourne and be with his family again: "It's great to

be back, I've settled in and caught up with a lot of old friends that I haven't seen in a while," he says.

Life in the public eye...
A life which is led in the public eye is, of course, never a hassle free one. When Alex dined out with old *Factory* colleague and friend, Andrew Daddo recently, he was continually harangued by fans, "Andrew was really good and said to them 'Look, we just want to be by ourselves'."

Another symptom of soap stardom is gossipy press stories and in the past, papers have even linked Alex and Kylie, something which he dismisses as an absurd rumour!

The truth is, that currently, Alex Papps is not seeing *anyone* and if he was it would probably be the most closely kept secret in the biz. However he *is* hoping to get married at some point in his life and when he does it will be a far cry from the circumstances under which Frank and Bobby were married: "I think that they rushed into it all without any proper understanding of each other. Frank sees marriage as a partnership where he is going to be strong, the big provider, the breadwinner. It's a chauvinist view..."

And on the subject of his own marriage; "I want to be a lot older before I commit myself. My parents have a happy marriage and that's what I want." ◄◄

THE PRIVATE FACE OF

NICOLLE DICKSON

Tragedy...

Behind Nicolle Dickson's professional exterior lies a true life story that makes the plot of *Home and Away* look positively tame. When she was eighteen she was involved in a near fatal car crash: "I fell asleep at the wheel and broke my jaw and cheekbones on the steering wheel... after being in hospital they had to wire up my face on the inside of my mouth. It was horrible!"

In addition to the physical pain that Nicolle suffered, there was also the psychological trauma. "My self esteem went completely downhill. I couldn't go to college and I couldn't go to castings."

Followed By Success...

Nicolle proved her resilience however, by making a full physical recovery and, with some parental persuasion, she started to attend auditions again. One of the auditions was, of course, *Home and Away*. Nicolle wasn't optimistic. There were nearly four hundred actresses competing for the role of Bobby Dickson...

But when casting directors told her that she had been successful she was overwhelmed, "I couldn't believe it, " she said. "It was like a Hollywood drama: I have a crash, I feel like I've wrecked my life, I want to give up and then this script comes along and I suddenly get to be famous!"

And Stardom...

All this is a long way in the past now and Nicolle has indeed, "got to be famous". (So famous that she needs her own personal bodyguard.) Her comments on this are characteristically modest: "When people say I'm a star I say, `No I'm not, I'm an actress. I live in the western suburbs... I like going out for walks by myself.' Someone like Laurence Olivier was a star, not me!"

Snap Happy...

Like Alex Papps, Nicolle's ambitions didn't always centre around acting. In fact, like him, she wanted to be a photographer. Before the crash episode she was studying visual arts at the Sydney School of Arts. Although she was side tracked into drama somewhere along the line she still has a passion for taking pics and has her own darkroom.

"I like doing shots that show some kind of emotion or feeling, "she says. "I keep meaning to do some shots of the Home and Away cast but I just haven't got round to it!"

Nothing Like Bobby...

One thing that is often picked up on in interviews with Nicolle is how completely different she is from her screen character, Bobby. Not only is she more mature and more independent but she is much more reserved than the forthright Bobby. She lives at home with her parents and likes to keep her private life well and truly private. As she told Eithne Power (TV Times magazine) last year, "The last time I mentioned in an interview that I had a boyfriend, he was no longer my boyfriend by the time the stuff got into print."

The Future...

So what does the future hold for Nicolle? When she was asked what she envisaged doing at the age of fifty she replied unhesitatingly, "Still acting, I'll have kids and I'll be in love!" Acting is clearly Nicolle's main passion despite the fact that she does tend to be very self-critical, ("Whenever I watch myself on screen there's so much I would change about my performance. Often it's just a little thing like I'll blink too much, but it can make a world of difference!") As for marriage, she says that's something that lies ahead and although she has recently become engaged she says, "I'm not getting married until at least my late twenties." ◄◄

> " Part of Bobby's popularity is because she does all the things other people wish they were brave enough to do. "

NICOLLE

● *Her bedroom at home is a converted garage.*

■ He is a descendant of Elizabeth Fry, the prison reformer.

● *Before Nicolle signed with* Home and Away *she had never set foot outside Sydney.*

■ He has a *Betty Blue* film poster on his bedroom wall.

■ He processes all his own photographs in a darkroom underneath the family house.

● *She used to go out with a male model called Andrew. "He's much, much taller than me and he's gorgeous," she said at the time.*

■ He loves sashimi and sushi.

● *Her dad's a truck driver.*

20 LiTTLe KnOWn FACTS...

■His family keep pet ducks.

●*She hates olives!*

■He has duck eggs for breakfast!!

●*Her favourite singer is David Sylvian.*

■He can't dance!

●*Nicolle once dyed her hair blonde but hated it and dyed it red!*

■He likes being sent flowers and he loves watching really romantic films!

●*Nicolle's ideal man is someone who is affectionate, honest and never paranoid!*

■He makes collages out of photographs of his friends and he reckons that they're "pretty groovy".

●*At the age of fifteen Nicolle studied drama and singing with the Keane Kids Company.*

■He relaxes by bashing away at his old piano and "doing a bit of singing".

●*Nicolle has had roughly three days off in the past year!*

ALEX

35

"I don't have a girlfriend at the moment. I suppose the old cliche is that I go for personality. I don't think it's fair to limit yourself to one sort of person. I've never had a *type* that I'm attracted to."

Nicolle on Going Out:
"One of the things I really enjoy doing is going to listen to a band or going to a club because the people there either don't know much about me being in *Home and Away* or they just don't care."

Alex on Make Up:
"It's amazing what a bit of make up and good lighting does. If you get harsh lighting it shows up every little pimple and hair."

Nicolle on Roo:
"The character of Bobby has always felt intimidated by Roo because she's so beautiful and sexy. She knows Frank has always fancied Roo and can't help suspecting that he's marrying Bobby on the rebound."

Alex on Fan Mail:
"I get my share of female fan letters - nothing spectacular so far. Usually they just ask for photographs."

Nicolle on Being Noticed:
"I never thought that people would notice me when I'm out in public. I thought that because I'm so short and I wear glasses off-camera, nobody would notice me."

Nicolle on Old Friends:
"My schoolfriends aren't fazed by what I've done. They know I'm still Nicolle and they're really pleased for my success."

Alex on Neighbours:
"*Neighbours* paved the way for *Home and Away* in England and though there are things that are better in *Home and Away* we are two very different series and I wish them well."

Nicolle on the British Press:
"I'm nervous. The press have been a bit unkind to Kylie and Jason. I don't want to be hounded like that."

Alex on the Environment:
"I'm very concerned about the natural environment. We have a big problem in Sydney with lots of companies dumping sewage and chemicals into the sea and polluting the beaches. It's dangerous for the swimmers as well as the fish."

Nicolle on Setting An Example:
"I'm really glad the scriptwriters have allowed Bobby to go on being a tomboy. She doesn't conform to what men think a woman should be and I think she's a good example to girls who watch the show."

Alex on Stock, Aitken and Waterman:
"It's disposable pop but it's fun and happy and if people get something out of it then that's great."

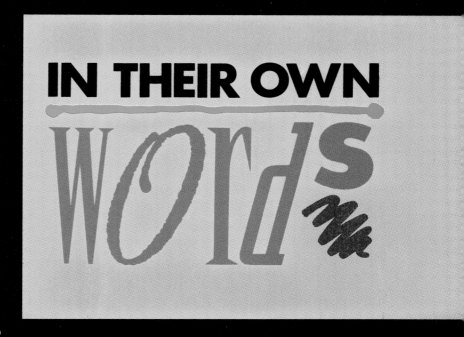

IN THEIR OWN WORDS

Nicolle on Marriage:
"I think the person you eventually marry should be your best friend as well as your lover, otherwise you haven't anything solid to build on when the first flush of passion's over."

Alex on Not Being An Actor:
"If the acting hadn't worked out I think I would have gone on to do some job in films or TV. Or maybe I'd have done journalism."

Nicolle on Autographs:
"I don't mind it when people ask me to sign my name. After all it's not much to ask. But I hate it when they don't even talk to me or say hallo."

Alex on Screen Kisses:
"It's a bit embarrassing at first but you get used to it. I guess it's easier to do those kinds of scenes where I come from than it is in England because the weather's better there and you don't get chapped lips!"

> **"** Amanda and I are very close, I'm a lucky guy. **"**

Q. Where did he grow up?
A. *In Dorrigo, Coff's Harbour.*

Q. How old is he?
A. *Twenty three.*

Q. What were his childhood ambitions?
A. *To be a policeman or a lawyer. "I would never have thought of being an actor. I come from the country - people don't do that sort of thing!"*

Q. So how come he's not walking the beat on Coff's Harbour?
A. *Well, it all started when he accompanied his sister to a modelling agency. The agency recognised his talent and snapped him up. At the age of fourteen he was working on campaigns for McDonalds, Coke, Pepsi and Wrigley.*

GREG BENSON *MATT*

Q. What about the famed Levi ad.?
A. *This was probably the one that really catalysed Greg's acting career. He was chosen from over one hundred models to do the Oz version of Nick Kamen's Levi 501's commercial. The simple act of taking off his jeans to reveal a pair of white boxer shorts made Greg a household name. He says, "I'm pretty sure that if I hadn't been in the Levi's ad, I would have never got the part in* Home and Away.*"*

Q. So, has he now renounced the life of a country boy?
A. *No - he currently lives in Umina, "I prefer to live there, where I can go fishing and surfing and diving rather than live in the city and have nothing to do!"*

Q. Who is Greg's favourite *Home and Away* character?
A. *"I really like Martin."*

Q. Does he reckon he's a sex symbol?
A. *"Sex symbols are older guys. You always think of them as being some sort of Hollywood star. Not someone of my age."*

Q. Is Greg `romantically involved' with anyone?
A. *Yes! It seems that* Home and Away *has given rise to a serious romance here! Apparently Amanda Newman Phillips decided that Greg was the man for her on her first day on the Summer Bay set as Narelle. And he must have felt the same way as the two have been going strong for quite some months now. Says Amanda, "I always fancied Greg, he's the nicest guy I've ever been out with."*

Q. Is it true that they are recording a single together?
A. *Possibly - at the moment they have just completed a demo. tape and are taking it around record companies. Their songs are described as love ballads with "a disco beat".*

Q. What is it like now that Alex Papps (Frank) has gone?
A. *Greg claims that Alex was different from the rest of the cast. "We used to muck around and have a laugh but Alex is quite quiet. He's not a bloke's bloke - he wouldn't go out with the lads for a few drinks."*

Q. What does the future hold?
A. *Greg plans to hang around Summer Bay for a while yet, but he also hopes for success in the pop world!*

When *Home and Away* hit our screens in the UK many moons ago what were the critic's first impressions? Was it just another blue-skied Oz soap or was it the "culturally valuable" social commentary that Alan Bateman yearned for?

"If I were connected with *Neighbours* I'd be a bit concerned about the future right now!" *(An insider from Oz TV.)*

"The constant moral lessons are relieved by the programme's wonderful Australianess for which the British seem to have such a soft spot." *(Minette Marrin, journalist.)*

"When *Home and Away* started, I said the only thing in it that played its part well was the sea.... livelier than any of the actors and prettier than any of the studio sets!" *(Hilary Kingsley; journalist.)*

"Tom and Pippa have got a hell of a job on their hands. Not only have they got to carve out a life for their six foster kids in a run down caravan park on the south coast, they've got to do it at the same time of day when, for centuries, people have sat down to watch the news!" *(Morris Gleitzman: humorist.)*

"The opening titles are standard emotional triggers - sunset, weepy love song, seagulls, glittering waves, a lovely smile... Nobody ever seems to draw real blood and so far I haven't seen any real wickedness. In this sense it is trivial... but then why not?" *(Minette Marrin.)*

"This is a soap opera which does not shy away from teenage desires. It debates and explores them in a very frank way." *(Ian Brandes, journalist.)*

"What we have here is a cross between *Grange Hill* and the *Waltons* and since it is bound to be tremendously successful, it is a cross we shall have to bear!" *(Peter Paterson, television critic.)*

"*Home and Away* producers have latched on to a magic formula - romance, weddings, babies and marriage break ups!"

"It's a heady combination of sun, sea, surf and scandal - how can it possibly miss?" *(Erica Goatley, journalist.)*

WHAT THE
CRITICS SAY

"I like watching Home and Away. That's the new Australian soap opera and it's better than Neighbours but maybe that's just because it's new!"
(Sarah Wadd from Hither Green).

"My favourite show is Home and Away, but Roo is a total cow and wrecks the whole show. She is always cheeky and gets away with it... she should be fired."
(Richard Henry from Basildon, Essex).

"The best characters are Bobby and Mr Fisher. They really crack me up. And Carly... she plays the part of an alcoholic really well. As for Lance, they should just write him out. I'm serious, he's rubbish!"
(S.M. Powell, from Peckham).

"We've got far too many Australian soaps on TV. I don't think this one's any better or worse."
(Esther Deadman from Orpington).

"I'm a real soap freak. If you could put Kylie Minogue and Jason Donovan in Home and Away it would be brilliant."
(R.C. Hiorns from Pratts Bottom).

"I really enjoy Home and Away. It's the best programme of its kind and not half as depressing as Eastenders."
(Clive from south west Scotland).

"Bobby's really good, she just doesn't care what anyone thinks of her. Home and Away is one of the better soaps from down under."
(Malcolm Langton from Stockwell).

We did our own mini survey to find out how the soap from down under was going down with the people who really matter... the viewers!

"It's compulsive viewing. You can't not watch it!" (Jacqui Sparrow from Finchley).

"Everyone used to rush back from college to see Neighbours. Now it's Home and Away." (Mary Forrest from East London.)

"I watch Home and Away, because, although it's boring, I sometimes want to know what's going to happen."
(Chris Larkins from Chipping Sodbury).

"I only started watching it a month ago but it's really easy to get into the story. It's a good programme."
(Lydia Bannister from Elephant & Castle).

"I used to love Prisoner Cell Block H. It was really mega. I have to say Home and Away isn't in the same league."
(Sue Murray from Birmingham).

"The characters are brilliant. You can really believe in Carly and Bobby."
(Audrey Pink from Kent).

"It's got a younger appeal than Neighbours. It's more like an Australian Grange Hill in that respect."
(Louise Cox from Twickenham).

"I can't understand the fascination with Home and Away and Neighbours. I watched Home and Away once and it was just totally melodramatic."
(Hany Sadek from Brixton).

WHAT THE VIEWERS SAY...

KATE

At the tender age of ten, fame has not swelled Kate Ritchie's head. In fact it has been said that she prefaces all her interviews with the line, "I'm nothing special."

But the signs are that she is *everything* special! This is the child who appeared in TV commercials at the age of five, who wrote, produced and directed her school play at the age of eight and who had the child lead in the mini-series, *Cyclone Tracy.*

If the word `precocious' springs to mind it wouldn't be unreasonable but as Katie would retort: "I'm not a star, I'm just lucky." And she goes on, "I don't really want to be an actress when I grow up. It's fun now but I think I'd rather be a landscape gardener or an author!"

One of the hardest bits of acting that Kate has had to do for the soap was "acting to thin air", when she had to shoot scenes with her imaginary friends `Milko' and Mr. Haggis. When asked how she portrayed those scenes convincingly she replied that she imagined that her seven year old sister Rebekah was in front of her and she would direct all the lines at her.

As well as Rebekah, Kate has two other siblings, Stuart, who is six, and Susan, three. But rather than being in awe of their older sister they take her fame very much for granted: "They aren't in the least bit impressed that I'm on television," says Kate. "And my parents don't treat me any differently. I still have to go to my room if I'm naughty!"

"If they wrote me out of *Home and Away* I'd cry!"

RITCHIE

SALLY

A PROFILE ON
JUSTINE CLARKE

ROO

AGE: Eighteen.

BACKGROUND:
Justine's mother, Beverley Clarke, is a dancer and actress, while father, Len, is a singer.

TV ROLES:
Professor Poopsnaggle, Maestro's Company, Willing and Able, Touch The Sun, Mad Max III and *A Country Practice*. Justine has also appeared in TV commercials since the age of seven.

FAVOURITE SINGER: James Brown.

FAVOURITE ACTOR /ACTRESS:
Cary Grant and Katherine Hepburn.

FAVOURITE PLACE: Kuta Beach, Bali.

FAVOURITE *HOME AND AWAY* CHARACTER: Celia.

LOVES:
Sunbathing and sleeping!

HATES:
Bank queues and weak cappuchinos!

JUSTINE ON *NEIGHBOURS*:
"I love *Neighbours* and watch it all the time. I used to love Jason, but that was when I was fifteen... I've grown out of him now."

JUSTINE ON MARRIAGE:
"Getting married when you're young and pregnant just makes for complications. Especially when you're not sure whether you love the person. I couldn't even think of getting married at the moment."

JUSTINE ON PLAYING ROO:
"I know everyone hates her. Once we did this promotion...everyone else was cheered while I got booed! You can't afford to take it all seriously."

CLASSIC ROO LINE:
"He's not going to go for you! Have you looked in the mirror? God, what a dag you are!" (To Bobby!)

THE FUTURE:
"When I finally finish up with *Home and Away*, I would like to go over to America and work there."

ALL ABOUT
ROGER OAKLEY

TOM

□ He's in his mid forties and as yet, unmarried!

□ He was born and brought up in New Zealand. He describes his young life as an "ordinary suburban upbringing". He has a sister who currently lives in Auckland with her three daughters.

□ Roger's interest in acting started when he was studying languages at a New Zealand University.

□ He did a part time drama course in Britain and he went to live and work in Australia in 1978.

□ He has been a professional actor for twenty years and his career has encompassed both TV and theatre roles. Everything in fact from *The Sullivans*, *Ground Zero*, *The Alchemist* and *The Norman Conquests*.

□ The part of Tom in *Home and Away* is Roger's longest acting job. On landing the part he said; "I've always felt I can play a wide range of roles. But I thought that from the way I was developing I was simply a character actor and the wrong type for a major TV role. But this is what they call a big break!"

□ His hero is Alec Guinness, "I admire his ability to almost disappear into a character. That sort of acting appeals to me. I like to feel I'm more like the character I'm playing than myself."

□ At some stage Roger would like to have kids and he claims he would consider fostering children. "Doing that," he says, "would be just as acceptable as having a child of my own, but obviously it would have to be just as acceptable to the other half. I've worked with kids on stage but I've seldom played a family man. It's great to have kids around you because they're such individuals!" ◀◀

> " Without being big-headed, I think I'm a good actor. "

A PROFILE ON

CRAIG THOMSON

ACTING:

In the past Craig has been a part time member of various drama schools; the main one being The Australian Theatre for Young People. *Home and Away* is Craig's first TV role. As he says, "Adam and I just went along to the auditions and got the parts, there's not much to tell really."

WHAT IT'S LIKE TO PLAY MARTIN:

"The public think I'm going to be a yob just because Martin is. You have to keep yourself in control and be nice to people. If you snub them, sooner or later it will come back on you."

PREVIOUS JOBS:

Craig has something of a chequered past when it comes to jobs. He's tried his hand at everything from boxing to being an apprentice green keeper!

OFF SCREEN:

Craig is a big fan of British punk rock. His hero is Sid Vicious, his favourite band is *The Sex Pistols* and his favourite film is *Sid and Nancy*. When *Public Image Ltd.* played in a Sydney stadium, Craig, of course, was there: "I always manage to get myself in trouble, but I *had* to go to see John Lydon!"

Other off screen pastimes include eating out, playing squash and watching cartoons. Craig is sometimes labelled the `alternative Australian' because he never sets foot on a beach and he can't surf!

BEYOND *HOME AND AWAY*:

There is a possibility that Craig may follow in the current soap trend of becoming a pop star. As he says, "I've been singing for about six years, my stuff's pretty sort of commercial rock, it'll have keyboards too. I might be doing some things with an English bass player and hopefully I'll release an album this year!"

MARTIN

tha
REFERENCE

NICOLLE DICKSON ON BOBBY:
"Sometimes I want to scream at Bobby and say, `For God's sake, don't be stupid. Can't you get your act together?'"

CRAIG THOMSON ON MARTIN DIBBLE:
"Martin's completely over the top, and very different from the rest of the cast. I really like playing comedy."

PETER VROOM ON LANCE SMART:
"Lance is definitely a drinker and if it wasn't for the timeslot he would be into marijuana too!"

JUSTINE CLARKE ON ROO STEWART:
"I know Roo is a cow but she does suffer!"

GREG BENSON ON MATT WILSON:
"Matt - he's well sure of himself!"

FRANK LLOYD ON NEVILLE MCPHEE:
"He was decent, friendly, good living and someone who helped everyone else. I liked him very much."

SHARYN HODGSON ON CARLY MORRIS:
"She's a bit of a sad case. The poor girl's demented or at least she will be soon. I feel sorry for her."

ADAM WILLITS ON STEVEN MATHESON:
"He's not the trendiest guy in the world, but thankfully as time passes he gets a bit wayward."

VANESSA DOWNING ON PIPPA:
"She's everyone's idea of a straight speaking, generally good hearted person."

ROGER OAKLEY ON TOM FLETCHER:
"Tom's a good character. He's got a bit of a short fuse but he's a really nice guy. He's a bit of a softy!"

PETER VROOM

LANCE

After leaving school at the age of 16, Peter worked as a ferry hand, a dispatch rider, a builder, a barman and a motor mechanic! Finally, he `fell' into acting and after a couple of years at the Australian Theatre for Young People he landed the role of `Lance'.

OFF SCREEN:

Peter's leisure pursuits are many and varied, but his biggest passion is probably aviation which he studied at University. He got his pilot's licence last year and flys "whenever I get the opportunity."
Peter's favourite actors and actresses include Meryl Streep, Nicolle Dickson and Mel Gibson.

THE FUTURE:

To a large extent Peter reckons that soaps are a training ground for actors and actresses: "I want to progress in this profession and go on to play other roles," he says. He is worried however, about the dangers of being typecast, "When you have a really strong image in a soap you can have a hard job finding other work."
When Peter is asked whether he will still be in the acting profession at the age of fifty (he is twenty one at the moment) his glib reply is, "No, I'll be working in the Stock Exchange by then!"

> "I want to make a distinction between me and my character. I get too much abuse from yobbos!"

THE

Home and Away ™

CHALLENGE

1. To find the younger members of the cast how many auditions did the *Home and Away* producers sit through?
a) 90.
b) 350.
c) 280.

2. What is Adam Willit's favourite thing about London?
a) The red buses.
b) The pigeons in Trafalgar Square.
c) The shops.

4. Nicolle Dickson's bedroom at home is somewhat unusual. Is it...
a) A cellar.
b) A converted garage.
c) A summer house.

3. What prop did Roo use to make her appear pregnant?
a) A pillow.
b) A bag of lentils.
c) An inflatable cushion.

5. Before *Home and Away*, what was Greg Benson famous for?
a) *Modelling Levi's.*
b) *His musical talent.*
c) *His starring role in* Young Doctors.

6. Vanessa Downing has a Masters degree in…
a) *Astrophysics.*
b) *Theatre studies.*
c) *English literature.*

7. In which country does Justine Clarke hope to work in the future?
a) *America.*
b) *England.*
c) *France.*

8. What would Alex Papps have been if he hadn't become an actor?
a) A teacher.
b) A dancer.
c) A journalist.

9. Which Neighbours character has defected to Home and Away?
a) Henry.
b) Harold.
c) Bronwyn.

10. What is Sharyn Hodgson's worst fear?
a) The supernatural.
b) Cockroaches.
c) Heights.

11. Where does Peter Vroom see himself at the age of fifty?
a) Playing Hamlet!
b) Cruising round the world.
c) Working in the Stock Exchange.

12. Who is Craig Thomson's hero?
a) *Sid Vicious.*
b) *Clive James.*
c) *Alec Guinness.*

13. Who is Nicolle Dickson's favourite singer?
a) *Paul Weller.*
b) *Jason Donovan.*
c) *David Sylvian.*

14. Which series is Alex Papps moving to?
a) *Flying Doctors.*
b) *Neighbours.*
c) *Prisoner Cell Block H.*

15. Where was Roger Oakley born and brought up?
a) *Austria.*
b) *New Zealand.*
c) *Canada.*

ANSWERS

15. **b** New Zealand.

14. **a** *Flying Doctors.*

13. **c** David Sylvian.

12. **a** Sid Vicious.

11. **c** Working in the Stock exchange.

10. **b** Cockroaches.

9. **a** Henry.

8. **c** A journalist.

7. **a** America.

6. **c** English literature.

5. **a** Modelling Levi's.

4. **b** A converted garage.

3. **b** A bag of lentils.

2. **c** The shops.

1. **b** 350.